THE
USBORNE
OFFICIAL
Roman
Soldier's
HANDBOOK

First published in Latin in 123AD by Brutus Books Ltd.
This edition published in 2014 by Usborne Publishing Ltd.,
Usborne House, 83-85 Saffron Hill, London EC1N 8RT, England.
www.usborne.com
Copyright © 2014, 2009, 2004 Usborne Publishing Ltd.

THE
USBORNE
OFFICIAL
Roman Soldier's HANDBOOK

Written by
Lucia Fabricius Imperiosa
(also known as Lesley Sims)

Illustrated by
Spurius Hostilius Bibulus
(also known as Ian McNee)

A survival guide for the raw recruit

CONTENTS

CHAPTER V

CHAPTER VI

Military expert: Dr. Boris Rankov

With thanks to the Ermine Street Guard,
a society dedicated to researching the Roman Army,
for providing the commands on pages 34-35.

Designed by Mike Olley and Ian McNee
Cover design by Stephen Moncrieff and Jamie Ball
Digital manipulation by Mike Olley and Louise Bartlett

CHAPTER 1

GETTING STARTED

Welcome, legionary, to the proudest, most professional army in the Western World. It's thanks to the army that our empire is the size it is. You've a tough life ahead but you'll make good friends, travel the world and be rewarded for your efforts with money and land when you retire. (Assuming you live that long. Just a little army joke to start things off.)

If this book belongs to someone else and you're reading it to see whether army life is for you, check the list of requirements below.

You must:

I. BE AT LEAST 1.75M (5'8") TALL

You'll be measured in bare feet, so don't think you can bring trick shoes.

II. BE SLIM BUT MUSCULAR

– being super-fit helps. Don't worry if you're not fit at the start of basic training. You will be by the end.

III. HAVE EXCELLENT VISION...

...AND HEARING

IV. BE ABLE TO READ AND WRITE

If you're holding this, you can probably read, but how good's your lettering? Army life's not all sword-slashing, you know – there's some pen-pushing too.

V. BE A ROMAN CITIZEN

You'll need proof – and a home-made toga from an old bedsheet isn't enough.

Think you'll satisfy the entrance board? Then there's only an interview and medical to pass before you're in. But there are other qualities not mentioned on recruitment posters that could prove useful – see the quiz below and overleaf.

CAMP CHARACTER: A QUIZ

Study the parchment below and then answer the questions to see if you've got what it takes to be a Roman soldier.

QUALITIES
PATRIOTIC, LOYAL,
NOBLE, JUST,
COURAGEOUS, SERIOUS,
GODS-FEARING,
DISCIPLINED

I. Your twin brother turns against Rome: would you kill him?

II. You've made a bad mistake and brought shame upon your family: would you kill yourself?

III. You've been fighting a war for five years. Finally, you win. Do you make friends with the defeated army?

IV. Your commander gives what you think is a ludicrous order which will lead to certain death. Do you obey him instantly?

V. You're defending a bridge against an entire army. When it is finally destroyed, could you then jump into the river, fully armed and swim back to Rome?

If you answered "YES!" to all five questions, what are you waiting for? Find someone already serving to recommend you and join up today. You'll swear a simple oath of allegiance and the next 25 years of your life belong to the army.

But where do you fit in?

ARMY ORGANIZATION

Where are you? At the bottom. You and seven other soldiers make up a contubernium, the smallest unit in the Roman Army. The largest is a legion with 5,120 soldiers. Think of contubernia* as bricks building the army. However many men there are in total, they all start out in groups of eight.

8 soldiers = a contubernium

8

8× 10

10 contubernia = a century

80

80× 6

6 centuries = a cohort

480

80× 10

10 centuries = a prima cohors

800

480 ×9

9 cohorts + 1 prima cohors = A LEGION!

+ 800

5,120

* plural of contubernium

Fellow recruits stand out: they're exhausted and sweating, like you. But in case other uniforms are confusing, here's a spotter's guide to...

WHO'S SHOUTING AT ME NOW?

Nº. I THE LEGATE: commands the legion, always a senator, and hand-picked by the emperor himself. Unless you're spectacularly good (or bad), your paths won't cross.

Legate

Nº. II TRIBUNES: six officers, led by a senior tribune – the legate's right-hand man. The other five are equestrian tribunes, in charge of paperwork and junior to the praefectus castrorum.

Senior tribune

Nº. III THE PRAEFECTUS CASTRORUM: third in command and in charge of building camps when the army's on the move.

The P.C.

Nº. IV THE PRIMUS PILUS: the most senior centurion around camp, he's the chief of the five senior centurions who command the prima cohors. He's also the most senior officer likely to get involved in any fighting. So give him respect.

Primus pilus

Nº. V THE CENTURION: in charge of a century and your immediate boss. Just pray you don't get landed with the infamous "Bring me another!" – so-called because he beats recruits until his cane snaps, when he cries (you guessed it), "Bring me another!"

Centurion

Nº. VI THE OPTIO: the centurion's second-in-command. Keep in with him. He'll report your every move to his boss.

Optio

Nº. VII THE TESSERARIUS: who gives out the daily password. Forget it and you won't be allowed back on base.

Tesserarius

Nº. VIII THE LEGIONARY:

another name for
an ordinary
footsoldier –
in other
words:
YOU!

Humble
legionary

Nº. IX THE AUXILIARIES: non-citizens from the provinces, grouped into cohorts of 500 to 1,000 men. They earn less than legionaries and get less training – but act as messengers and scouts, as well as fighters.

Auxiliaries on the battlefield
fight in loose formation.

Auxiliary

Cavalry soldier

Nº. X THE CAVALRY SOLDIER: on horseback and in the minority. Traditionally from the aristocracy (since connections and money were vital), but now drawn from the wider empire.

Nº. XI THE CORNICEN: the horn blower who helps you march in time. He also plays musical orders, such as "Eat!" If you don't want to starve (and to avoid a beating), pick the tunes up early on.

Cornicen

Two men hard to miss are the standard bearers, who carry troops' various emblems into battle.

AQUILIFER: bears the legion's standard, topped with the noble Roman eagle (aquila).

If the standard is lost in battle, your entire legion will be in disgrace (and serious trouble).

Aquilifer

Signifer

SIGNIFER: seen here carrying the standard of a maniple, or pair of centuries. (Maniple means "handful" hence the hand.) He's also in charge of the burial club. Pay up weekly and you're sure of a decent funeral.

Watch out for the pointed tips: they're sharp.

HANGERS ON

Soldiers are only some of the hundreds of people involved in keeping the army marching. Just because not all of the following fight, doesn't mean they're any less crucial. (Well, yes it does, but don't say that to their faces. You might need them one day.)

PRIEST (OR SEER)

In dire straits, praying may be all you have left.

CLERK

In charge of admin, meet the camp's Official Penpusher.

SURVEYOR

The man who plans forts and camps.

(It's not that hard a job, since all forts and camps follow a similar layout.)

DOCTOR

If things get this far, you'll just have to grin and 'bare' it.

THE OPPOSITION

That's it for the guys on your side, but who might you be facing?

Before you go on to read about the joys of basic training, here's a spotter's guide to...

THE BARBARIAN ENEMIES OF ROME

I. GERM-RIDDEN GERMANICS

* farmers and herders
* small groups of warriors serve a chief
* their land is handy for Gallia (north-west Europe) and full of iron
* to wind them up, grab their women and cattle

Long, unwieldy sword

Flat shield

No protective clothing

Chainmail
tunic

Deadly
spear

II. DEADLY DACIANS

* large army, equipped
with war machines

   * warriors trained
   in our fighting
   techniques by
   Roman fugitives,
   who are given a
   haven in Dacia

III. GALLUMPHING GAULS

* less war-like than
   Germanics
* VERY
   superstitious
* rely on
   priests called
   Druids to
   help them
   win battles

Vulnerable
bare feet

Beats sword against shield

IV. COLD CELTS

* very tall with shaggy, bleached hair
* often fight naked, making weird, harsh shouts to unnerve opponents
* cut off the heads of victims and nail them above their doors

V. PARTHIAN PRANKSTERS

* the trickiest, most dangerous enemy
* horse-archers fire hundreds of arrows on the move so they can't be hit
* will flee and then round on pursuers

CHAPTER II

LIFE OF A RAW RECRUIT

You'll soon know most people around camp, at least by sight. But you'll get to know the seven soldiers in your contubernium better than brothers. The most experienced one of you will be boss and, just so you don't forget, your contubernium will take his name.

Basic Training: for the first four months, you'll eat, sleep and breathe nothing else. New recruits are out twice a day – in wind, rain, hail or fog – perfecting battle drills, handling weapons and getting fit.

Just singin'
and marchin'
in the rain...

The eventual aim is for you all to react as one almost before the centurion barks his order. Remember: the army fights as a single unit.

EVERY SOLDIER
MUST KNOW

I. WHAT TO DO
II. WHEN TO DO IT

ALL TOGETHER NOW!

Acting in unison is probably one of the hardest things you'll have to master. But don't worry. An ingenious exercise has been devised which combines working as one with keeping fit: the ROUTE MARCH...

On a normal route march, you'll cover 20 Roman miles (that's almost 30 kms and just over 18 miles) in five hours. But if your centurion is having a bad day – and he usually is – he could make you march as far as 24 Roman miles (35.5 kms; 22 miles) in the same time.

Take earplugs on marches.

Tone-deaf cats sound more tuneful.

You'll be sent on a route march about once every ten days. Singing rhythmic songs with fellow marchers can help you keep in step. (The words are much too rude to print here but you'll pick them up quickly enough.)

WHOLE KIT & KABOODLE

What makes a route march so bad is that you carry everything you'd take if you were moving camp. In fact, you often march somewhere, set up camp and take it straight down again. This isn't because your centurion can't make up his mind but so you get used to putting up tents in a flash. (See pages 88-90.)

IN THE BAG

The combination of pack plus weapons can weigh over 30kgs (70lbs). Imagine carrying a large dog on your back for five miles.

As we often say in the army: weight training? Who needs it?

BLOODLESS BATTLES: THE DRILL

When you're not marching or recovering on your bunk, you'll be on the parade ground, working on drills and fake fights to learn how to handle weapons. You'll start with fake weapons: wooden swords and wicker shields, twice as heavy as the real thing, to build up strength.

If that sounds easy, try thrusting a heavy sword at a 1.8m (6ft) high wooden post. When you've cracked that, run up first.

You'll also be jumping forward, back, side to side, up and down... You may feel more like an acrobat than a soldier, but these moves all help to develop three vital fighting qualities:

I. Strength

II. Stamina

III. Agility

MARCHING ORDERS

In training and battle, centurions constantly bark instructions at you. The sort of commands you're likely to hear are listed below.
Learn 'em or weep:

AD SIGNA (Fall in)

INTENTE! (Atten-tion!)

LAXATE (Stand at ease)

PROCEDITE
(Forward march)

DEXTRORSUM VERTITE (Right turn)

SINISTRORSUM VERTITE (Left turn)

RETRORSUM VERTITE (About turn)

CONSISTITE (Halt)

SALUTATE (Salute)

GLADIOS STRINGITE
(Draw swords)

GLADIOS RECONDITE
(Sheath swords)

PILA IN TERRAM
(Put javelins in ground)

PILA SUMITE
(Pick up javelins)

SCUTA TOLLITE (Raise shields)

SCUTA DEMITTITE (Lower shields)

ITER ACCELERATE (Speed up)

ITER TARDATE (Slow down)

EXPECTATE... (Wait for it...)

AB SIGNIS DISCEDITE! (Dismiss!)

TRAINING TREADMILL

Of course you might spend 25 years' service without seeing any battle action at all. You may even stay in the same garrison (army base) for your entire career.

Halt! Who goes zzzz...

You might ask:

If I'll never fight, why's the training so tough?

Answer: Just in case. You must always be ready – you could be needed at any moment.

Besides, as every centurion knows, the only way to get an instant response – not to mention unquestioning obedience – is through harsh training.

No centurion is ever without his cane, worn down from continually beating legionaries.

Which brings us to...

DISCIPLINE

THE ROMAN ARMY'S TOP FIVE PUNISHMENTS

In fifth place it's those:

V. BEATINGS

In fourth place,
this will have you exhausted:

IV. EXTRA FATIGUES (CHORES)

Coming in at number three
– and handy for dieters:

III. GOING WITHOUT RATIONS

Second, for theft or desertion (and getting more
drastic) is:

II. BEING BEATEN TO DEATH

But none can topple the worst one of all. Yes, at number one, for cowardice, comes:

I. DECIMATION

Get stuck in a cohort where someone runs away in battle and ten percent of the cohort has had it. Back at camp, lots are drawn and one out of every ten men is executed.

Even without actual wrong-doing, you'll need to keep up high standards to please your centurion. And they're arbitrary creatures. If one takes a dislike to you, you'd better make a speedy sacrifice to Mars, God of War.

PLEASING THE BOSS

Or you could try bribery. All officers accept bribes, usually from men hoping to escape unpleasant duties. The good news is you will receive a regular wage, so bribes can come out of this.

A vital move:
the back-hander.

As a legionary, you'll get a basic 300 denarii a year (far better than a craftsman). Auxiliaries get slightly less; cavalrymen slightly more. But, as you go up the ranks, so does your pay.

A junior officer, such as a tesserarius, has pay and a half. A senior officer, such as a signifer, is on double pay. Centurions are on 4,500 denarii – before bribes – and the primus pilus has a whopping 18,000.

Don't think being a soldier is a "Get rich quick" option. While food and clothes are organized by the army, you'll have to pay for them.

WHO GETS A PIECE OF THE PIE?

Bribes

Burial fund

Spare cash

Food

Clothes, bedding and weapons

You'll pay for your weapons too – a good reason to look after them. Let your sword get rusty and a chunk of spare cash will go on replacing it.

Last, though not least, there's the burial fund. This will cover the full cost of your funeral should the worst happen – including burial, tombstone and a feast for the mourners – so you can rest in peace.

FREE & SINGLE...

But what's left after that is all yours. There's a
ban on soldiers marrying. If you were married
already, the marriage was annulled when you
enlisted – which you might want to tell your wife.

(Actually many soldiers keep families in
civilian quarters outside the forts. The state
just pretends they don't exist.)

PROMOTION & PATRONAGE

After a few years, if you want a promotion you'll need an influential relative (a patron). Ask him to write a letter saying how wonderful you are and you'll shoot up the career ladder on greased boots. You could try to impress your boss with a bold battle move instead (not so easy if there's no war and you're simply on guard duty).

Sucking up...

...or dusting down

KEEP IT IN THE FAMILY

On the whole, promotion is gradual and rises
to higher ranks take generations to happen.

Great-granddad, a
humble legionary

Dad, a
primus pilus

Me, a
legate

My son, the
emperor?!

CHAPTER III

READY FOR A FIGHT?

This chapter is where the real soldier stuff starts. From weapons to uniform, you'll find out what you get issued with and how to use them. What are you waiting for? Get to it!

WEAPONS OF ATTACK

ARE YOU THINKING LIKE A SOLDIER YET?

A quick question to begin. You're about to go into battle. Which of the following would you take as ATTACKING weapons?

I. PILUM (JAVELIN)

Wooden shaft (can be up to 120cms or 4ft long)

Main stem of flexible iron (60-90cms or 2-3ft), long enough to go through shield and body

Sharp barbed point

II. GLADIUS (SWORD)

Scabbard (cover)

Inside, the sword's blade (60cm or 18in long) is of the best-quality steel.

Long straps, so you can hang it from your shoulder

III. PUGIO (DAGGER)

Rounded at tip

Scabbard

The dagger's blade is made of iron or bronze.

IV. SCUTUM (SHIELD)

Stands
120cms
(48in) high

Held together
by an iron rim

Bulge
known as
a "boss"

Curved to
provide
excellent
body
coverage
and deflect
missiles

70cms
(28in) wide

Made of solid layers of wood and leather,
shields can weigh up to 10kgs (22lbs).

So which weapons would you take?
You might be surprised to learn that all
four can be used for attack, even the shield.

* If you thought a shield was only used to hide behind, check page 59. It's a useful weapon in its own right.

* And if the dagger was your first choice – it's only there for back-up and used mainly for chores.

Now for a look at them in more detail...

THREE THINGS TO KNOW ABOUT A PILUM

I. The iron rod goes in deeeeeeeeep.

II. Once it hits a shield it won't come out.

III. It bends on hitting the ground (so the enemy can't throw it back).

IMPORTANT THING ABOUT A GLADIUS

A legionary always wears it on his RIGHT
(even if he's left-handed). Think about it:
in battle you fight shoulder to shoulder, so
everyone must draw from the same side.

Before long,
your gladius
will feel like
an extension of
your right arm.

HOW TO DRAW YOUR SWORD

I. Grab the handle,
with your thumb
pointing down.

II. Grasping
it firmly,
pull out the
sword.

III. Once it's
clear of its
cover, point it
up and out.

HOW TO USE YOUR SWORD

Slashing at an enemy might not hurt him enough if he's covered up. Besides, it leaves you open to attack under your slashing arm. Remember:

A THRUST BEATS A SLASH

Bring your sword back and...

...thrust it between your enemy's ribs.

HOW TO HOLD YOUR SHIELD

Hold on your left, with an overhand grip.

This grip makes your shield easier to carry.

Shield cover

The cover has straps so you can carry it on your back.

HOW TO USE YOUR SHIELD AS A WEAPON

The bulging "boss" in the middle of the shield
is like having an iron fist, so you can:

PUNCH THEN STAB

When the enemy is near...

...smash the boss into him and follow up with a swift
sword thrust.

UNIFORM

So much for weaponry. What about combat gear?
Well, first is the tunic.

Short sleeves

Embarrassingly
short
skirt

The tunic is made from linen or wool,
depending on where you're stationed
and how hot – or cold – it gets.
    Of course, a tunic gives you no
protection from attack whatsoever...

...so over it you'll wear a mail vest, with leather pads on the shoulders. The alternative is a lorica segmentata, a metal breastplate held together by leather strips.

Mail vest

Leather pad

Lorica segmentata

Overlapping iron strips give better protection.

Underneath you wear bracae, or wool leggings, for the cold. Leg guards, known as greaves, would be useful too, but they're only for officers (to show their superior rank).

Bracae
(can itch)

Metal greaves

Leather
straps tie
around
legs.

Then there's the helmet, not entirely failsafe with large parts left uncovered. And it's heavy. (Imagine wearing a fat frozen chicken on your head.)

Leather strings tie under chin.

Hinged guards protect cheeks.

Inside fittings are attached with rivets, so helmets are lined with wool or linen padding. This quickly gets worn from dirt and sweat, so replace it regularly.

Going from top to toe, on your feet you'll wear sandals, aka caligae. They're hard-wearing enough for marches, but you only get three pairs a year, so look after them.

They're designed not to rub, but grease new pairs with oil.

The soles are studded with hobnails for rough terrain and gripping on grass.

Don't worry if you're posted somewhere cold and damp. For murky, miserable Britannia, you'll get a pair of boots like these.

For travel and cold nights on guard duty, you'll get a wool cloak (which can double as a blanket). You also get a scarf so your uniform doesn't rub your neck.

Finally, you'll wear a cingulum militare, a belt which has studded leather strips hanging down the front. It won't give you any extra protection, but it does jingle as you walk, so people know you're coming and get out of the way.

Hang your sword from here.

The extra strip of leather may save your blushes: those tunics are short!

You can add campaign tokens (badges from battles) to personalize your belt.

A simple sum:

I bent pilum + II sloppy sandals
   = I bad soldier

Your uniform doesn't have to gleam on parade (unless the emperor's around), but it must protect you in battle. Metal rusts quickly, especially in damp countries, so:

KEEP IT WELL GREASED!

Keep all your leather well-greased too: not only
will it last longer, it will also be more flexible. Olive
oil or animal fat – with plenty of elbow grease –
should do the trick.

To shift rust, make a paste of
sand and oil or fat and rub in well.

CHAPTER IV

LET BATTLE COMMENCE!

Roman soldiers are renowned for two things: their ferocity in battle and their absolute refusal to surrender. But, before the battle even starts, there are various tricks you can use to knock the enemy off-balance.

BATTLE TRICKS

I. KEEP THE SUN AT YOUR BACK

Any glare
will blind
the enemy.

II. CHECK THE WIND DIRECTION

If it's blowing away from you, dust will fly into the
enemy's faces, causing coughing, confusion and
chaos. Missiles will go further too.

III. GRAB A HEIGHT ADVANTAGE

If there's a hill, make sure you're on top.

By the time the enemy soldiers have staggered up to meet you, they'll be sweating, exhausted and in no state for combat.

BATTLE TACTICS

I. THROW THEM BEFORE THEY THROW YOU

To unnerve the enemy
from the start, advance
slowly and in
ABSOLUTE
SILENCE.

When your massed ranks are about 15m (50ft)
away, hurl your pila* and charge forward with
swords drawn, screaming a battle cry as you go.

II. STICK TOGETHER

Give the enemy no chance to break through your
ranks and, if they don't run from your terrifying
charge, try hand-to-hand combat.

* plural of pilum

III. USE BATTLE FORMATIONS

THE SAW:

Keeps a unit immediately behind the front line, which can move to block any holes.

Front line

Hole in front line

Moving in to block the hole

THE WEDGE:

Enemy
ranks

Breaking through
the enemy ranks

Form a triangle, with one
soldier at the tip. Thrust
into the enemy, then
spread out.

This neat move gives the enemy no
room to swing their long and, let's
face it, frankly unwieldy swords.

THE ORB (A CIRCLE):

A defensive position and the last resort. Only form this if completely outnumbered.

It's a fight you'll lose – but you'll go down fighting.

THE TESTUDO (OR TORTOISE):

Form a rectangle, holding your shields over your heads, or before you if you're at the front. This creates an almost impenetrable barrier and is especially useful in a siege (see pages 82-84).

The tortoise is so strong, a cart could be driven over the top.

THE SKIRMISH:

Simply a widely spaced line-up, giving you more room to fight – though it does also give the enemy more chance to penetrate.

IV. GET IN BATTLE ORDER

Everyone has a set place to stand when they line up for battle, carefully designed so weaker troops can be supported by stronger ones. One possible battle line-up is shown below.

2nd line

Elite troops   Trainees   Selected troops   Trainees   Good troops

The boss

Elite troops   Weak troops   Average troops   Weak troops   Average troops

Front line

OMENS

Of course, none of the above is any use if the gods aren't on your side. Your commander should check for encouraging signs before he gives the order to fight. Here are some of the signs to look out for:

* feeding sacred hens (if they eat, attack)

Yes!!

* checking entrails (leave this to the seer)

* seeing an eagle
   in the sky (could
   be good, could
   be bad)

You can help
with sacrifices and
sending up the odd
prayer to Mars.

VICTORY PROCESSION

Standard bearers followed by centurions

Last (and least), you

The emperor (daubed in red to show he is almost a god)

Remember: you're only a man!

A servant stands behind the emperor, to ensure he doesn't get big-headed.

A tradition loved by emperors and sportsmen alike, after a triumphant battle comes the glorious parade.

This is your chance to enjoy fifteen minutes of fame, drinking in the cheers. Feel free to hurl the odd insult at the emperor, as he acknowledges the crowd. It's thought to bring good luck.

Cheering crowd (which doesn't hurl insults, on pain of death)

Twelve men known as lictors carry rods (symbols of authority).

Captured loot

Prisoners of war (who'll be sold as slaves or killed)

Animals for sacrifice

Senators and other important politicians - who don't fight but are happy to share the glory - grab the lead.

SIEGES

Of course, you won't always face your enemy on the battlefield. Sometimes they hole up in town and refuse to leave. Luckily, starving them out is a thing of the past, thanks to useful technology invented by the Ancient Greeks.

SIEGE TOWER

Drawbridge

A simple yet ingenious design of a tall enclosed tower. It carries dozens of soldiers under cover up to the tops of the city walls. A drawbridge at the top of the tower lets the soldiers out.

BATTERING RAM
An effective way to break through the main gate, inside there's a tree trunk suspended from ropes.

MECHANICAL CROSSBOW
Large and stationary but can fire two bolts at once.

"SCORPION" CATAPULT Used to fire bolts and deadly accurate.

THE ONAGER (or "Wild Ass") CATAPULT Too large to use on a battlefield, this throws massive rocks over 300m (900ft).

Height-adjustable sling

DONE ANY CARPENTRY?

...because before you can fire the siege engines, you have to build them. Do this away from the city to be safe from enemy fire.

HOW LOW (DOWN & DIRTY) CAN YOU GO?

Try screwing up the enemy by:

I. firing the severed heads of spies over the walls;

II. building a second ditch and wall around existing ones. This not only stops help from reaching the city, it reminds the rebels they're trapped.

AFTERMATH

Once you've broken through, it's all over bar the shouting (massacring and looting). Your commanders will have given the besieged every chance to surrender before the attack. If they held out at the first hit of the ram:

GIVE NO MERCY!

You're not simply punishing them, you're warning other cities not to hold out too.

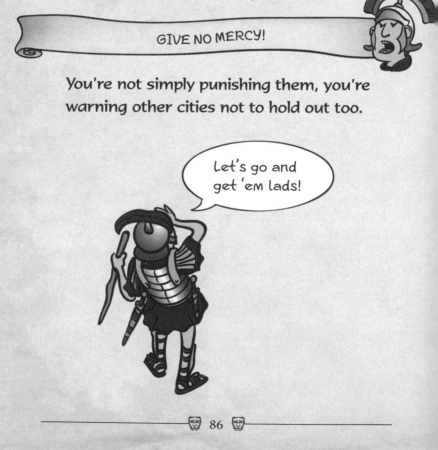

Let's go and get 'em lads!

CHAPTER V

CAMPS, FORTS AND HADRIAN'S WALL

With such a vast empire to defend, you could be sent anywhere from Syria (hot) to Britannia (not). But you'll soon feel at home because all camps and forts are built in a similar pattern.

SETTING UP CAMP

Camps have two purposes:

    I. to keep you safe,

    II. to impress the enemy. Seeing an entire tent village go up in next to no time is enough to unnerve anyone. It helps that everything is always in the same place.

A centurion's tent

Contubernium's tent

Supper break

Where to pitch your tent

via decumana

via principalis

via praetoria

Headquarters

Unloading supplies

Pitching a tent

Building the fence

Key:

Legionaries

Auxiliaries

Cavalry

Officers

Legate's HQ

Horses and mules

Fence

You'll dig a ditch around the outside and stick in stakes to keep unwelcome visitors out.

FORGOTTEN ANYTHING?

The tents are loaded on baggage carts or mules. You'll carry everything else. To make sure you don't leave anything behind, check the list below.

PACK CHECKLIST

- UNIFORM ☐
- WEAPONS ☐
- POTS AND PANS ☐
- FOOD RATION ☐
- BEDDING ☐
- PERSONAL BELONGINGS ☐
- TWO STAKES FOR FENCE ☐

FRONTIER FORTS

When you're not on the move, you'll live in a permanent base on the edge of the empire. Forts pretty much follow the layout of camps, though with plenty of added extras, such as stables, foodstores, workshops, latrines, a bath house, bakery and hospital.

Plan of a fort for 800 men

Key:

- ■ Ditch
- □ Rampart
- ■ Headquarters
- ■ Barracks
- ■ House of commanding officer
- ■ Granaries (foodstores)
- ■ Workshops and hospital

via decumana

via principalis

via praetoria

A QUICK TOUR INSIDE A FORT: THE ARMY HQ

The headquarters, or principia, is the main office and bank for the camp. The most precious things are housed here: the legion's standard, a bust of the emperor – and your wages.

Cross hall (or basilica) where you'll gather for orders

Notices are pinned on the other side of this wall. Keep an eye out for important announcements, such as inspections.

Records
room

Chapel (with
permanent
guard)

A ROOM IN A BATH HOUSE

Every fort has comfortable baths where you can take a dip and relax with friends. You'll find they're like bath houses everywhere, with hot and cold baths and a massage room – just what you need to unwind after a heavy day on the parade ground.

THE GRANARY (STOREHOUSE)

If an army marches on its stomach, you certainly
won't go hungry – granaries are kept full of
grain, huge joints of meat and plenty
of vegetables to build up energy
not only for route marches
but all those drills.

Unloading
sacks of grain

THE COMMANDER'S HOUSE

While you're squashed in tiny barracks, your commanding officer, together with his wife and family (he gets to keep his), can really spread out. In fact, most commanders' houses take up easily a tenth of any fort. This is his official residence though, so it's also used to host banquets and house visiting VIPs.

Main bedroom

Chapel

Slaves' toilets – these are more sociable than the commander's. He has to go alone.

The commander's private office

Bathroom

Dining room

Kitchen

Stable with a yard next door

Waiting room

Your quarters are much more basic but at least they won't let in rain (unlike tents). Each contubernium shares a pair of rooms in one of the long, narrow barrack blocks.

Weapons

Smelly feet

The biggest problem is snoring but balls of candle wax make good earplugs.

Sleeping quarters are at the back, with the weapons store in front. You'll have a small brazier for heating, if you're somewhere cold, but that's it.

FORT LIFE

You won't spend much time sleeping anyway. From the moment the bugle blows at dawn, you'll be up and hard at work. The question is:

ARE YOU A MILES OR AN IMMUNIS?

As a new recruit you'll probably be a miles and get the worst tasks: guard duty (boring) or cleaning – the principia, the bath house or the latrines (enough said).

Without a trade, you'll be stuck scrubbing toilets.

There's a chance you may go on road patrol or do police work, but your safest bet is to get a trade or skill as soon as possible. As a skilled immunis, you'll escape the dirty jobs and instead could be a fighting butcher, blacksmith, engineer, clerk or vet.

WHAT'S UP DOC?

If you don't faint at the
sight of blood (and if you do,
why are you in the army?), you
could always be an army doctor.
Army hospitals are where Roman
medicine is learned. It's not hard, since
treatment is basic (though effective).
You'll mostly be setting broken bones or
hacking off limbs if they're too far gone to save.
But there's also a range of medicines at your
disposal. If all else fails, simply remind your
patient his health is in the hands of the gods.

ALL ROADS LEAD TO ROME...

...and most were built by the army. For a life in the open air, train as an engineer, stone mason or carpenter. The army always has some building project on the go.

Roads, especially, are essential for an army on the move, not to mention messengers and trade. Yet parts of the empire are so backward, they hardly have any roads at all. (And as for aqueducts carrying clean water – forget them. You can only assume the barbarians never wash.)

Stuck on road-building duty, you'll spend all day breaking up rocks or digging foundations.

Be warned: you'll have to build a mile (1,000 paces) every three days.

Roads are built up in layers, on a bank between two ditches.

Shifting slabs into place

When your legion reaches a river, you'll be building the bridge across it. There's a choice of two. Pontoon bridges, made of wood and resting on barges, can go up in days. If time isn't an issue, you'll be building in solid stone.

BUILD YOUR OWN FRONTIER

You could spend quite a lot of your time building things. Emperor Hadrian has stopped all expansion, deciding the empire's quite big enough. But he wants wooden forts to be rebuilt in stone, plus walls, fences and ditches to be built along the frontiers.

A milecastle (fortified gateway) on Hadrian's Wall

Milecastles are built along the wall every Roman mile.

Changing the guard

Keeping watch

LIVING ON THE EDGE

Browsing in
the market

Out with an
unofficial girlfriend

Cloth for
family back
home

Most forts along the edges of the empire
are well established – so settled, in fact,
that towns have grown up around them.
And there's no shortage of traders, keen
to talk you out of your wages.

FUN & GAMES

A town on the doorstep is especially useful when it comes to time off. You can spend a traditional day out, shouting yourself hoarse at a gladiator fight or the races. Or borrow a horse and head to the country for a hunt.

Being a chariot rider can be as dangerous as soldiering.

If you do go hunting, your prey will depend on where you're posted. Expect to chase bears or deer in a northern province – or leopards, lions and wild boar in Africa.

Here's your chance to get close to animals you may only have seen at the Colosseum.

But if that's too much action, try a show at the local playhouse, where you're guaranteed fake blood and a laugh.

ARE YOU BEING SENT OVERSEAS?

Don't panic if you're posted a long way from home. Just read these useful tips to make your stay more fun.

* Find out about the native gods and include them in your prayers and sacrifices just in case. You don't want to start offending local deities.

* Share Roman customs, such as roads and bathing, with the natives, but don't be closed off to their traditions. OK, some natives paint themselves before battle. War paint may suit you.

* As for the weather, all you need remember is: Africa's hotter, Britannia's wetter.

* Get friendly with a messenger and arrange for relatives to send you the occasional package from home. There are bound to be several things you miss.

* Be prepared to learn the local language. You may be here for the next 25 years.

* Find out which natives are friendly – and which ones aren't (mostly the ones on the wrong side of the frontier).

CHAPTER VI

HANDY REFERENCE

Annual Legionaries
vs Centurions Quiz

I f you're put on the spot by an officer asking
tricky questions, whip out this chapter. Covering
army history, tactics and who ruled when, it also
has a map of the empire so you can see where the
bad guys are coming from. And at the very end
there's a quiz to test your new-found knowledge.

A HISTORY OF THE ARMY
(WITH THE BORING BITS LEFT OUT)

The Roman Army's strength is largely thanks to the sheer number of battles it fights. Here are a few highlights, beginning in the early republic when there was hardly an army at all.

FIGHTING FARMERS

c.510BC on: Soldiers are property owners (often farmers). Wars are near Rome and brief.

c.396BC: Soldiers are paid for the first time.

340BC: Wars move away from Rome, which means the farmer-soldiers have to leave their farms for longer. The soldiers are still handier with a hoe than a sword. Only the rich citizens can afford weapons and protective clothes.

387BC: Gauls from northern Europe attack and invade Rome.

350BC: The army tries to pull itself together.

343-290BC: The Samnites, a tribe from central Italy, decide Rome is getting too strong and three wars with them follow.
Rome also defeats an alliance of Latin cities.

280-275BC: The Pyrrhic Wars – battles with an army led by King Pyrrhus of northern Greece over a Greek city in Italy.

264BC on: The famous Punic Wars with the city of Carthage on the North African coast begin.

264-241BC: 1st Punic War means building a navy.

218-201BC: 2nd Punic War, begun by Hannibal, a Carthaginian general governing the Carthaginian territory of Spain. Hannibal leads an army of 35,000 men and 37 elephants over the Alps. Taken by surprise, the Roman army suffers a crushing defeat. Hannibal wins a lot of fights.

ROMAN GENERALS START COPYING HANNIBAL

202BC: Hannibal is finally defeated by Scipio, a Roman commander.

149-146BC: 3rd Punic War – Carthage destroyed.

107BC: Marius, a soldier and politician, becomes a Roman consul and introduces army reforms:

* Anyone can join
* Soldiers have the same weapons and training
* Troops carry their own equipment, so they can travel faster
* The legions are organized into ten cohorts
* The eagle becomes the only standard of the Roman legion

THE ARMY BECOMES WHAT IT IS TODAY

88BC: Sulla, Marius's former lieutenant, is made a consul and picks a fight with Mithridates, King of Asia Minor. Marius is given command of the army. Sulla is furious and marches on Rome.

88-66BC: Mithridates is equally cross. Three wars follow.

73-70BC: The slaves in Italy are crosser. The army is called in to quell their rebellion.

60BC: Two ex-consuls, Pompey and Crassus, form an alliance with newcomer Julius Caesar.

58-50BC: Caesar conquers Gaul.

55 + 54BC: Caesar invades Britain.

54-53BC: Crassus invades Parthia – a big mistake, as he's defeated and killed.

49-45BC: Caesar and Pompey argue. Civil war breaks out.

44-42BC: Caesar is assassinated by Brutus and Cassius, leading to another civil war, this time beween them and the team of Mark Antony and Octavian, Caesar's adopted son.

42BC: Brutus and Cassius lose. Mark Antony and Octavian divide Roman territory into East and West. Mark Antony moves in with Cleopatra, Queen of Egypt. Tension grows between Octavian and Mark Antony.

31BC: The sea battle of Actium – Octavian defeats Mark Antony.

27BC: Augustus, formerly known as Octavian, becomes emperor, starting the Roman Empire.

BIRTH OF IMPERIAL ARMY; THE INVASIONS GO ON

43AD: Claudius launches invasion of Britain.

58-64AD: More wars with Parthia.

60AD: Britons, led by Boudicca, rebel and are defeated.

66-74AD: The Jews rebel but are only defeated after eight years of fighting and sieges.

68-69AD: Emperor Nero's death means civil war.

70sAD: Britons cause trouble.

86-106AD: On and off battles with the Dacians for twenty years, which the Romans finally win.

113-117AD: Buoyed up by victory, Emperor Trajan decides to fight the Parthians and expands the empire to its greatest extent.

117-138AD: Emperor Hadrian says the empire is big enough and stops all invasions. He begins a massive building scheme on the frontiers.

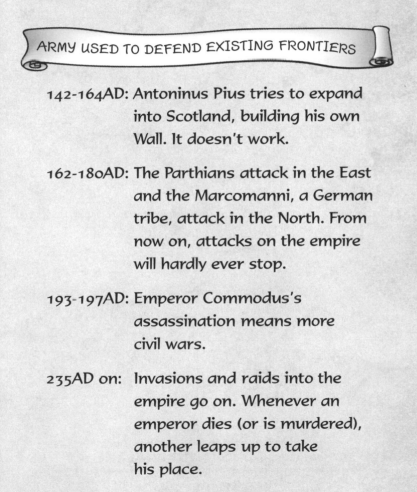

ARMY USED TO DEFEND EXISTING FRONTIERS

142-164AD: Antoninus Pius tries to expand into Scotland, building his own Wall. It doesn't work.

162-180AD: The Parthians attack in the East and the Marcomanni, a German tribe, attack in the North. From now on, attacks on the empire will hardly ever stop.

193-197AD: Emperor Commodus's assassination means more civil wars.

235AD on: Invasions and raids into the empire go on. Whenever an emperor dies (or is murdered), another leaps up to take his place.

BATTLE PLAN

As a rule, tactics are the concern of your commander, but it might help to have at least a vague idea of what's going on in his head. These diagrams show a typical and popular battle plan.

1. The cavalry attacks the enemy's cavalry, while the front line of legionaries advances to break up the enemy front line.

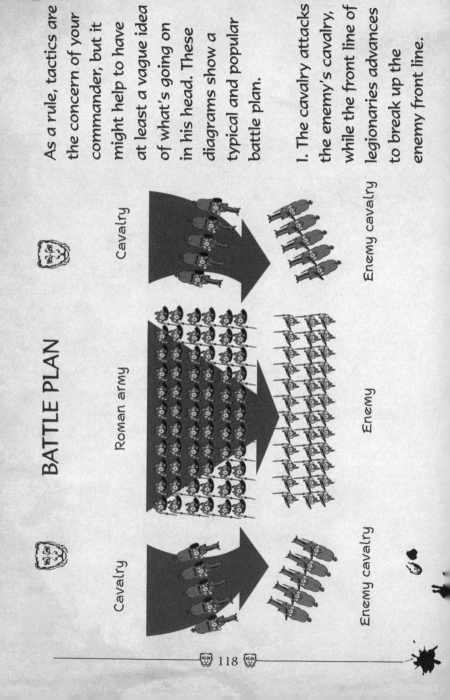

Cavalry

Roman army

Cavalry

Enemy cavalry

Enemy

Enemy cavalry

11. The second line of legionaries moves in, to fill any gaps appearing in the enemy's ranks. Meanwhile, the cavalry regroups and now attacks from the sides and rear. The enemy cavalry retreats.

Cavalry

Enemy cavalry

Roman army

Enemy

Cavalry

Enemy cavalry

WHO RULED WHEN – THE EMPERORS

It won't spoil your promotion prospects in the least to have a few names and dates at your fingertips. Memorize this list, then show off your knowledge as the occasion demands.

27BC-14AD	Augustus
14-37AD	Tiberius
37-41AD	Caligula
41-54AD	Claudius
54-68AD	Nero
69AD	Galba; Otho; Vitellius
69-79AD	Vespasian
79-81AD	Titus
81-96AD	Domitian
96-98AD	Nerva
98-117AD	Trajan
117-138AD	Hadrian

A WORD ABOUT CAESAR

Don't make the mistake of referring to Julius Caesar – one of the army's great heroes – as an emperor. He was a soldier, politician and writer, and in 46BC became the supreme ruler (or 'dictator') of Rome. But the empire didn't happen until almost 20 years after he was murdered in 44BC.

A FINAL QUIZ

SO, SOLDIER, WERE YOU PAYING ATTENTION?

A vital part of being a soldier is remembering what you've been told. Try this quiz and see just how much you remember.

 Six centuries make...
- a cohort
- a consort
- a concertina

 The optio...
- tests your eyes before a battle
- is the centurion's right-hand man
- is the best soldier in camp

 Legionaries wear their swords...
- on the left
- on the right
- whichever side they like

 A lorica segmentata is...
- a battle move
- a type of sandal
- a metal breastplate

A shield weighs...
- 1kg (2.2lbs)
- 10kgs (22lbs)
- 100kgs (220lbs)

When fighting, keep the sun...
- above you
- in front of you
- behind you

The onager catapult is...
- ideal for the battlefield
- only for use in sieges
- small enough to fit in a pack

ANSWERS

I. Six centuries make a cohort.
II. The optio helps the centurion.
III. Legionaries wear their swords on the right.
IV. A lorica segmentata is a metal breastplate.
V. A shield weighs 10kgs (22lbs).
VI. When fighting, keep the sun behind you.
VII. The onager catapult is only for use in sieges.

INDEX